Revision

Maths and English

Paul Broadbent,

Peter Patilla and

Louis Fidge

**Age 8–9
Year 4**
Key Stage 2

Hachette UK's policy is to use papers that are natural, renewable and recyclable products and made from wood grown in sustainable forests. The logging and manufacturing processes are expected to conform to the environmental regulations of the country of origin.

Orders: please contact Bookpoint Ltd, 130 Milton Park, Abingdon, Oxon OX14 4SB. Telephone: (44) 01235 827720. Fax: (44) 01235 400454. Lines are open 9.00a.m.–5.00p.m., Monday to Saturday, with a 24-hour message answering service. Visit our website at www.hoddereducation.co.uk.

© Paul Broadbent, Peter Patilla and Louis Fidge 2013
First published in 2007 exclusively for WHSmith by
Hodder Education
An Hachette UK Company
338 Euston Road
London NW1 3BH

This second edition first published in 2013 exclusively for WHSmith by Hodder Education.

Impression number   10 9 8 7 6 5 4 3 2 1
Year   2018 2017 2016 2015 2014 2013

Cover illustration by Oxford Designers and Illustrators Ltd
Illustrations by Fakenham Prepress Solutions, Fakenham, Norfolk NR21 8NN
Typeset in 16pt Folio by Fakenham Prepress Solutions, Fakenham, Norfolk NR21 8NN
Printed in Italy

A catalogue record for this title is available from the British Library.

ISBN: 978 1444 189 049

Contents

English

The *WHS Revision* series

The *WHS Revision* books enable you to help your child revise and practise important skills taught in school. These skills form part of the National Curriculum and will help your child to improve his or her Maths and English.

Testing in schools

During their time at school all children will undergo a variety of tests. Regular testing is a feature of all schools. It is carried out:

- *informally* – in everyday classroom activities your child's teacher is continually assessing and observing your child's performance in a general way
- *formally* – more regular formal testing helps the teacher check your child's progress in specific areas.

Testing is important because:

- it provides evidence of your child's achievement and progress
- it helps the teacher decide which skills to focus on with your child
- it helps compare how different children are progressing.

The importance of revision

Regular revision is important to ensure your child remembers and practises skills he or she has been taught. These books will help your child revise and test his or her knowledge of some of the things he or she will be expected to know. They will help you prepare your child to be in a better position to face tests in school with confidence.

How to use this book

Units

Each book is divided into a Maths section and an English section. Within each section there are twenty units, each focusing on one key skill. Each unit begins with a **Remember** section, which introduces and revises essential information about the particular skill covered. If possible, read and discuss this with your child to ensure he or she understands it.

This is followed by a **Have a go** section, which contains a number of activities to help your child revise the topic thoroughly and use the skill effectively. Usually, your child should be able to do these activities fairly independently.

Revision tests

There are two revision tests at the end of the Maths section and two revision tests at the end of the English section. These test the skills covered in the preceding units and assess your child's progress and understanding. They can be marked by you or by your child. Your child should fill in his or her test score for each test in the space provided. This will provide a visual record of your child's progress and an instant sense of confidence and achievement.

Parents' notes

The parents' notes (on pages 30–31 for the Maths section and pages 59–60 for the English section) provide you with brief information on each skill and explain why it is important.

Answers

Answers to the unit questions and tests may be found on pages 32–34 (Maths) and pages 61–64 (English).

Unit 1: Place value

⬤ Remember

The numbers between 1000 and 9999 all have four digits:
thousands, hundreds, tens and ones.
To make a number ten times bigger or smaller, you need to move the digits.

To multiply by 10:   To divide by 10:
move the digits one place to the left   move the digits one place to the right
and fill the space with zero

$$84 \times 10 =$$
840

$$730 \div 10 =$$
73

⬤ Have a go

1 Multiply each of these numbers by 10.

a $89 \times 10 \rightarrow$ ▢   b $76 \times 10 \rightarrow$ ▢   c $31 \times 10 \rightarrow$ ▢   d $92 \times 10 \rightarrow$ ▢

e $60 \times 10 \rightarrow$ ▢   f $314 \times 10 \rightarrow$ ▢   g $296 \times 10 \rightarrow$ ▢   h $488 \times 10 \rightarrow$ ▢

i $720 \times 10 \rightarrow$ ▢   j $897 \times 10 \rightarrow$ ▢

2 Divide each of these numbers by 10.

a $620 \div 10 \rightarrow$ ▢   b $810 \div 10 \rightarrow$ ▢   c $200 \div 10 \rightarrow$ ▢   d $470 \div 10 \rightarrow$ ▢

e $990 \div 10 \rightarrow$ ▢   f $1840 \div 10 \rightarrow$ ▢   g $3090 \div 10 \rightarrow$ ▢   h $7660 \div 10 \rightarrow$ ▢

i $8500 \div 10 \rightarrow$ ▢   j $6870 \div 10 \rightarrow$ ▢

3 Complete these chains. Look carefully at the signs.

a 746 ➡ + 10 ➡ ___ ➡ × 10 ➡ ___ ➡ − 100 ➡ ___ ➡ ÷ 10 ➡ ___ ➡ + 1 ➡ ___

b 397 ➡ × 10 ➡ ___ ➡ + 100 ➡ ___ ➡ − 10 ➡ ___ ➡ + 100 ➡ ___ ➡ ÷ 10 ➡ ___

c 980 ➡ + 100 ➡ ___ ➡ + 10 ➡ ___ ➡ ÷ 10 ➡ ___ ➡ − 10 ➡ ___ ➡ × 10 ➡ ___

4 Make up your own chain. Can you make the end number the same as the start number?

698 ➡ _ _ _ ➡ ____ ➡ _ _ _ ➡ ____ ➡ _ _ _ ➡ ____ ➡ _ _ _ ➡ ____ ➡ _ _ _ ➡ 698

Unit 2: Sequences

Remember

To work out the pattern in a sequence, we look at the difference between each number. Sequences can include negative numbers.

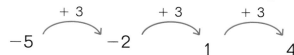

$-5 \quad \xrightarrow{+3} \quad -2 \quad \xrightarrow{+3} \quad 1 \quad \xrightarrow{+3} \quad 4$

The pattern or rule is **+ 3**.

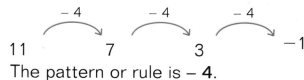

$11 \quad \xrightarrow{-4} \quad 7 \quad \xrightarrow{-4} \quad 3 \quad \xrightarrow{-4} \quad -1$

The pattern or rule is **– 4**.

Have a go

1 Continue these sequences and write the rule.

a   −12   −7   −2   3   _____   _____   _____   _____
Rule: _____

b   −9   −7   −5   −3   _____   _____   _____   _____
Rule: _____

c   −12   −9   −6   −3   _____   _____   _____   _____
Rule: _____

d   14   10   6   2   _____   _____   _____   _____
Rule: _____

e   50   40   30   20   _____   _____   _____   _____
Rule: _____

f   19   14   9   4   _____   _____   _____   _____
Rule: _____

2 Write the missing numbers.

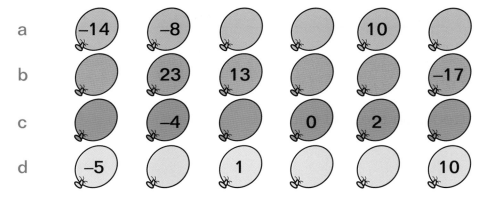

a   −14   −8   ⬡   ⬡   10   ⬡

b   ⬡   23   13   ⬡   ⬡   −17

c   ⬡   −4   ⬡   0   2   ⬡

d   −5   ⬡   1   ⬡   ⬡   10

Unit 3: Multiples

Multiples are like the numbers in the times tables, but they go on and on.
Multiples of 3 are: 3, 6, 9, 12, 15, 18, ..., 63, 66, 69 and so on.
Multiples of 4 are: 4, 8, 12, 16, 20, ..., 72, 76, 80 and so on.
Multiples of 5 are: 5, 10, 15, 20, 25, ..., 75, 80, 85 and so on.

Have a go

1 Look at these numbers.
Write them in the correct boxes. Be careful – some will be in more than one box.

68 75 40 54 30 85 48 60 52 27 120 90 100 45

Multiples of 3	Multiples of 4	Multiples of 5

Write the numbers that are multiples of 3, 4 and 5 from the list above:

_____

2

1	2	3	4	5	6	7	8	9	10	11	12	13	14	15	16	17	18	19	20
21	22	23	24	25	26	27	28	29	30	31	32	33	34	35	36	37	38	39	40
41	42	43	44	45	46	47	48	49	50	51	52	53	54	55	56	57	58	59	60
61	62	63	64	65	66	67	68	69	70	71	72	73	74	75	76	77	78	79	80
81	82	83	84	85	86	87	88	89	90	91	92	93	94	95	96	97	98	99	100

a Colour all the multiples of 3.

b Circle all the multiples of 4.

Look at the different patterns on the 100 grid.

Unit 4: Number puzzles

Remember

Maths puzzles can be quite tricky. Prepare for these by making a small set of 1–20 number cards from paper or thin card. Use these to practise with.

Have a go

1 Write 16 of the numbers on this grid so that they follow the rules.

For example, the top left-hand number must be a multiple of 3 and an odd number. So it could be 3, 9 or 15.

	multiple of 3	> 8	multiple of 5	any number
odd number				
multiple of 2				
< 12				
multiple of 4				

2 Write each of the numbers 1 to 20 in this Carroll diagram.

Be careful with the centre box – if a number is inside, it must be greater than 10.

	multiple of 3	not a multiple of 3
even number	> 10	
not an even number		

Unit 5: Rounding numbers

Remember

Rounding numbers – by changing them to the nearest ten or hundred – makes them easier to work with.

Rounding to the nearest 10
Look at the **units** digit.
If it is 5 or more, round up the tens digit. If it is less than 5, the tens digit stays the same.

345 rounds up to 350.
684 rounds down to 680.

Rounding to the nearest 100
Look at the **tens** digit.
If it is 5 or more, round up the hundreds digit.
If it is less than 5, the hundreds digit stays the same.

5763 rounds up to 5800.
3245 rounds down to 3200.

Have a go

1 Round these to the nearest 10.

a 756 ➡ _____   b 384 ➡ _____   c 149 ➡ _____   d 205 ➡ _____

e 744 ➡ _____   f 942 ➡ _____   g 1574 ➡ _____   h 6382 ➡ _____

i 8925 ➡ _____   j 3047 ➡ _____   k 7954 ➡ _____   l 2327 ➡ _____

2 Round these to the nearest 100.

a 463 ➡ _____   b 258 ➡ _____   c 145 ➡ _____   d 676 ➡ _____

e 607 ➡ _____   f 934 ➡ _____   g 6934 ➡ _____   h 1845 ➡ _____

i 8653 ➡ _____   j 2168 ➡ _____   k 3408 ➡ _____   l 2657 ➡ _____

3 Estimate these approximate answers. For example, for the first question you round 329 up to 330 and 192 down to 190 so the answer is 520.

a Round these to the nearest 10.

329 + 192 ➡ [520]

672 − 348 ➡ [   ]

37 × 29 ➡ [   ]

b Round these to the nearest 100.

4238 + 1209 ➡ [   ]

6854 − 2445 ➡ [   ]

429 × 481 ➡ [   ]

Unit 6: Fractions

◯ Remember

Fractions have a numerator and a denominator.

The numerator shows the number of the parts you are dealing with.

The denominator shows the number of equal parts.

$$\frac{1}{4}$$

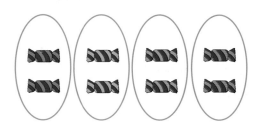

$\frac{1}{4}$ of 8 is the same as $8 \div 4 = 2$

◯ Have a go

1 Write the fraction of each amount.

Colour $\frac{1}{2}$ and write the answer.	Colour $\frac{1}{4}$ and write the answer.
a 👟👟👟👟👟👟 $\frac{1}{2}$ of 6 = _____	**d** 🍬🍬🍬🍬🍬🍬🍬🍬🍬🍬🍬🍬🍬🍬🍬🍬 $\frac{1}{4}$ of 16 = _____
b 🧁🧁🧁🧁🧁🧁🧁🧁🧁🧁 $\frac{1}{2}$ of 10 = _____	**e** 🍎🍎🍎🍎 $\frac{1}{4}$ of 4 = _____
c 🎁🎁🎁🎁🎁🎁🎁🎁 $\frac{1}{2}$ of 8 = _____	**f** ⚽⚽⚽⚽⚽⚽⚽⚽⚽⚽⚽⚽ $\frac{1}{4}$ of 12 = _____

2 Answer each of these.

a $\frac{1}{3}$ of…	**b** $\frac{1}{5}$ of…	**c** $\frac{1}{4}$ of…	**d** $\frac{1}{10}$ of…
12 ➡ _____	10 ➡ _____	24 ➡ _____	50 ➡ _____
9 ➡ _____	25 ➡ _____	40 ➡ _____	20 ➡ _____
21 ➡ _____	30 ➡ _____	28 ➡ _____	70 ➡ _____
18 ➡ _____	40 ➡ _____	20 ➡ _____	60 ➡ _____
15 ➡ _____	35 ➡ _____	36 ➡ _____	90 ➡ _____

Unit 7: Addition

◯ Remember

If you are given a sum and the numbers are too big to work out in your head, then you may need to use a written method.

Example: 537 + 258

❶ Write the numbers in a column, lining up the units digits.

```
 537
+258
```

❷ Start by adding the units column. Any total over 9 put the tens digit under the next column.

```
 537
+258
────
   5
   1
```

❸ Now do the same with the tens column. Keep going left until all the columns have been added.

```
 537
+258
────
 795
   1
```

◯ Have a go

❶ Work out the answers.

a
```
  347
+ 285
─────
```

b
```
  532
+ 189
─────
```

c
```
  624
+ 287
─────
```

d
```
  359
+ 386
─────
```

e
```
  257
+ 794
─────
```

f
```
  638
+ 527
─────
```

g
```
  463
+ 864
─────
```

h
```
  792
+ 688
─────
```

❷ Write in the missing numbers 1–9, using each number once only.

a
```
  □6 1
+7 □8
──────
 1 2 8 9
```

b
```
  3 6 4
+8 □6
──────
 1 2 4 0
```

c
```
  □5 7
+6 □□
──────
  9 7 5
```

d
```
  2 0 □
+ □□3
──────
  8 9 7
```

| 1 | 2 | 3 | 4 | 5 | 6 | 7 | 8 | 9 |

Unit 8: Subtraction

Remember

If you are given a subtraction and the numbers are too big to work out in your head, then you may need to use a written method. Try these two methods to work out 346 − 184.

Method 1

1 Write the numbers in a column, lining up the units digits.

```
  346
− 184
```

2 Starting from the right-hand column, take away the bottom number from the top number.

```
  346
− 184
────
    2
```

3 Now do the same with the other columns. If the top number is smaller than the bottom number, then, in this example, exchange a 10 from the hundreds column.

```
  ²3¹4 6
− 1 8 4
──────
  1 6 2
```

Method 2

Find the difference between the numbers by counting on.

1 Draw a blank number line.

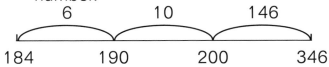

184   346

2 Count on to the next ten, then to the next hundred, then to the number.

```
      6         10        146
184       190        200        346
```

3 Add up all the jumps.
6 + 10 + 146 = 162

Have a go

1 Work out the answers.

a	b	c	d	e	f
834	655	297	656	725	907
− 217	− 384	− 148	− 378	− 456	− 488

2 Use the number line method for these.

a 578 − 369 = _____   b 635 − 284 = _____   c 732 − 581 = _____

d 642 − 488 = _____   e 913 − 769 = _____   f 804 − 387 = _____

Unit 9: Using brackets

Remember

When part of a calculation is in brackets, you work out the brackets part first. If there are no brackets, work out the sum in the order it is written.

13 − (6 + 5) = 13 − 11 = 2

13 − 6 + 5 = 7 + 5 = 12

Have a go

1 Answer these.

a
18 − (9 + 5) = ☐

b
16 − 7 − 4 = ☐

c
14 + 5 − 7 = ☐

d
16 − (9 + 3) = ☐

e
15 − (7 + 4) = ☐

f
7 + 9 + 4 = ☐

g
19 − (18 − 14) = ☐

h
17 − 9 + 8 = ☐

2 Answer these. Remember to work out the brackets first.

a
(13 − 9) + (11 − 5) = ☐

b
(15 − 6) − (3 + 5) = ☐

c
(16 + 8) − (9 + 6) = ☐

d
(19 − 6) − (7 + 4) = ☐

e
(13 + 8) + (11 − 6) = ☐

f
(19 − 12) + (14 − 8) = ☐

3 These calculations don't need brackets to make the answer 24, but the signs are missing. Write the missing signs.

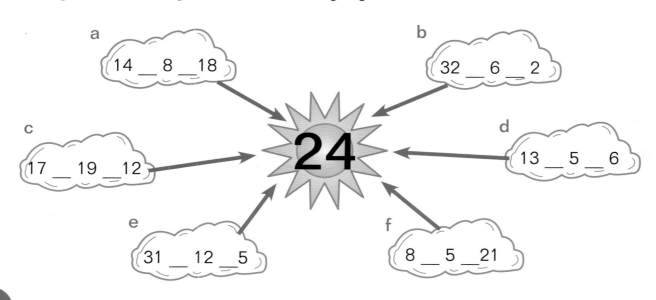

a 14 __ 8 __ 18

b 32 __ 6 __ 2

c 17 __ 19 __ 12

d 13 __ 5 __ 6

e 31 __ 12 __ 5

f 8 __ 5 __ 21

24

Unit 10: Multiplication

 **Remember**

If you know your tables, then it makes multiplying by multiples of ten much easier.

$4 \times 3 = 12$ $8 \times 5 = 40$

$40 \times 3 = 120$ $80 \times 5 = 400$

 **Have a go**

1 Use a timer. Answer these as quickly as you can.

a	b	c	d
$3 \times 8 = $ _____	$7 \times 5 = $ _____	$4 \times 6 = $ _____	$9 \times 3 = $ _____
$8 \times 6 = $ _____	$4 \times 9 = $ _____	$8 \times 7 = $ _____	$5 \times 10 = $ _____
$3 \times 6 = $ _____	$7 \times 4 = $ _____	$8 \times 9 = $ _____	$4 \times 5 = $ _____
$3 \times 7 = $ _____	$9 \times 9 = $ _____	$2 \times 8 = $ _____	$7 \times 6 = $ _____
$8 \times 4 = $ _____	$7 \times 7 = $ _____	$10 \times 8 = $ _____	$6 \times 9 = $ _____

Try it again. Can you beat your best time?

2 Complete these.

a $\times 5$	b $\times 6$	c $\times 7$	d $\times 8$
70 ➡ _____	50 ➡ _____	20 ➡ _____	40 ➡ _____
30 ➡ _____	40 ➡ _____	50 ➡ _____	20 ➡ _____
90 ➡ _____	80 ➡ _____	80 ➡ _____	60 ➡ _____
40 ➡ _____	60 ➡ _____	40 ➡ _____	90 ➡ _____
60 ➡ _____	30 ➡ _____	70 ➡ _____	50 ➡ _____

Unit 11: Division

Remember

If a division is a little tricky to work out mentally, you may want to use a written method instead.
Always work out an approximate answer first.
96 ÷ 6 is approximately 100 ÷ 5 = 20

Long method:
```
      16
   6 | 96
    −60  (6 × 10)
      36
    −36  (6 × 6)
       0
```
Answer: 16

Short method:
```
      1 6
   6 | 9₃6
```

How many 6s are there in 90?
6 × 10 is 60, with 30 left over.
How many 6s in 36?
6 × 6 is 36.
So 6 × 16 is 96. 96 ÷ 6 = 16

Have a go

1 Answer these.
Colour each star red if you worked it out mentally, or blue if you used a written method.

a ☆ 3 | 75

b ☆ 6 | 84

c ☆ 4 | 92

d ☆ 3 | 87

e ☆ 7 | 112

f ☆ 8 | 128

g ☆ 4 | 136

h ☆ 9 | 117

i ☆ 5 | 135

j ☆ 7 | 105

2 Write the missing digits for each of these.

a ☐ 7 r2
   5 | 8 ☐

b 2 ☐
   4 | ☐ 6

c ☐ 6 r ☐
   4 | 6 7

d ☐ 6
   6 | 9 ☐

e 1 ☐ r2
   7 | ☐ 6

Unit 12: Mixed calculations

The symbols for calculation are:

+ addition
− subtraction
× multiplication
÷ division

When part of a calculation is in brackets, you work out the brackets part first.

$(14 - 8) + (4 \times 3) = 6 + 12 = 18$

1 Choose from +, −, ×, ÷.

Complete these number statements.

a 7 ☐ 4 ☐ 3 = 31   b 12 ☐ 9 ☐ 4 = 7   c 15 ☐ 3 ☐ 6 = 18

d 3 ☐ 8 ☐ 3 = 21   e 6 ☐ 4 ☐ 6 = 30   f 18 ☐ 6 ☐ 5 = 8

2 These are a bit trickier!

a 4 ☐ (3 ☐ 6) = 36   b 5 ☐ (12 ☐ 7) = 10   c 6 ☐ (16 ☐ 4) = 24

d (4 ☐ 3) ☐ (3 ☐ 4) = 24   e (6 ☐ 8) ☐ (2 ☐ 5) = 4   f 5 ☐ (7 ☐ 2) ☐ 4 = 15

Unit 13: Money calculations

**Remember**

If money calculations are too difficult to work out in your head, you may need to work them out on paper instead.

When you add money amounts using a written method, make sure that you line up the decimal points.

$$\begin{array}{r} £\ 7.45 \\ +\ £\ 5.93 \\ \hline £\ 13.38 \end{array}$$

When you work out an amount of change, it is sometimes easier to count on. What is the change from £15.00 for an item costing £8.93?

£8.93 ➡ £9 is 7p.
£9 ➡ £15 is £6.
The change is £6.07.

Have a go

Look at this menu from a Chinese restaurant.

These are the orders from six customers. Work out the total cost of each and their change from £20.

新世界飯店	新世界飯店
Soup £2.27	Chicken chop suey £4.93
Prawn crackers £1.14	Chow mein £3.16
Spring rolls £1.85	Spare ribs £4.59
Beansprouts £2.59	Sweet and sour pork £4.08
Special fried rice £3.18	Chinese Garden special £5.69

a
Prawn crackers
Special fried rice
Spare ribs

Total cost: _____
Change from £20: _____

b
Soup
Beansprouts
Sweet and sour pork

Total cost: _____
Change from £20: _____

c
Chinese Garden special
Chow mein

Total cost: _____
Change from £20: _____

d
Chicken chop suey
Spring rolls
Special fried rice

Total cost: _____
Change from £20: _____

e
Sweet and sour pork
Spare ribs

Total cost: _____
Change from £20: _____

f
Prawn crackers
Chinese Garden special
Beansprouts

Total cost: _____
Change from £20: _____

Unit 14: 2D shapes

Remember

A **polygon** is any 2D shape with **straight** sides. The sides and angles of a **regular polygon** are all equal.

These are the names of some polygons.

Triangle	3 sides	△
Quadrilateral	4 sides	☐
Pentagon	5 sides	⬠
Hexagon	6 sides	⬡
Heptagon	7 sides	⬡
Octagon	8 sides	⬡

These are 2D shapes that are not polygons.

Circle	◯
Semicircle	◖
Oval	◯

Have a go

1 Name each shape.

a ⬡ [   ] b ☐ [   ] c △ [   ] d ⬡ [   ] e ◺ [   ] f ⬠ [   ]

g ⬡ [   ] h ◇ [   ] i ▱ [   ] j ◯ [   ] k ◖ [   ] l ◯ [   ]

2 Draw the shapes above on this Venn diagram.

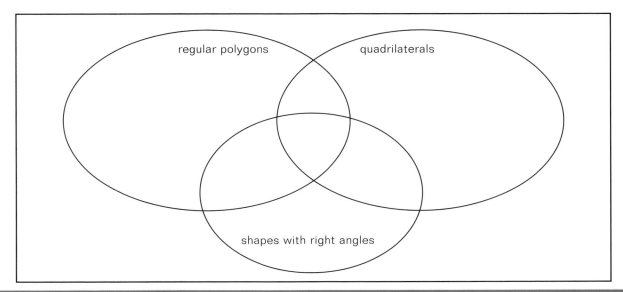

regular polygons   quadrilaterals

shapes with right angles

Remember

3D solids are solid shapes with three parts:
edges, faces and vertices (corners).

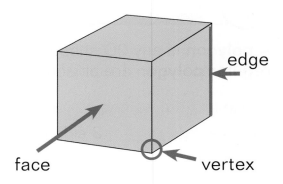

edge

face

vertex

A cube has 6 faces, 8 vertices and 12 edges.

Have a go

1 Name these shapes.
Write the number of faces, edges and vertices of each shape.

a

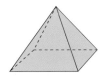

_____

___ faces ___ edges ___ vertices

b

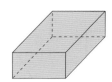

_____

___ faces ___ edges ___ vertices

c

_____

___ faces ___ edges ___ vertices

d

_____

___ faces ___ edges ___ vertices

2 Join each shape to the correct part of this Venn diagram.

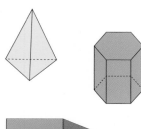

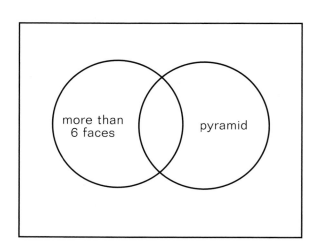

more than
6 faces

pyramid

Unit 16: Angles

⬤ Remember

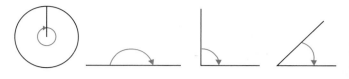

Angles are measured in degrees (°).
* A complete turn is 360°.
* Half a complete turn is 180°.
* A quarter turn is 90°, also called a right angle.
* Half a right angle is 45°.

⬤ Have a go

1 Put these angles in order of size, starting with the smallest.

a   A   B   C   D   _____

b   A   B   C   D   _____

c   A   B   C   D   _____

d   A   B   C   D   _____

e   A   B   C   D   _____

2 Use the clock face to help you complete this table. The angle of turn is for the hour hand.

Time	Clockwise angle of turn	New time
3 o'clock	90°	6 o'clock
1 o'clock	180°	
6 o'clock		9 o'clock
10 o'clock	360°	
	90°	8 o'clock
7 o'clock		10 o'clock
	180°	11 o'clock

Unit 17: Measures

● Remember

Length
1000 m = 1 km
500 m = $\frac{1}{2}$ km

100 cm = 1 m
50 cm = $\frac{1}{2}$ m

10 mm = 1 cm
5 mm = $\frac{1}{2}$ cm

Weight or mass
1000 g = 1 kg
500 g = $\frac{1}{2}$ kg

Capacity
1000 ml = 1 l
500 ml = $\frac{1}{2}$ l

● Have a go

1 Write these lengths.

a 2500 m = _____ km

b 6 km = _____ m

c 250 cm = _____ m

d 45 mm = _____ cm

e 12 000 m = _____ km

f 2050 cm = _____ m

g 14 cm = _____ mm

h 11 km = _____ m

i 2000 mm = _____ cm

2 Write these weights.

a 4000 g = _____ kg

b $3\frac{1}{2}$ kg = _____ g

c 1250 g = _____ kg

d 10 kg = _____ g

e 6500 g = _____ kg

f $5\frac{1}{4}$ kg = _____ g

g 3750 g = _____ kg

h $2\frac{3}{4}$ kg = _____ g

i 4500 g = _____ kg

3 Write these capacities.

a 4000 ml = _____ l

b 8 l = _____ ml

c 1500 ml = _____ l

d $2\frac{3}{4}$ l = _____ ml

e 4250 ml = _____ l

f 12 l = _____ ml

g 4750 ml = _____ l

h $4\frac{1}{4}$ l = _____ ml

i $2\frac{1}{2}$ l = _____ ml

Unit 18: Length – millimetres

Remember

Short distances can be measured in **millimetres**.

1 centimetre = 10 millimetres
1 cm = 10 mm

Have a go

1 Measure each of these lines in millimetres. (Don't include the spider!)

a _____ mm
b _____ mm
c _____ mm
d _____ mm
e _____ mm
f _____ mm
g _____ mm
h _____ mm

2 Answer the questions about the bugs.

a Who is 45 mm from B? ____

b Who is 27 mm from A? ____

c Who is 9 mm from E? ____

d Who is 34 mm from C? ____

e Who is 18 mm from F? ____

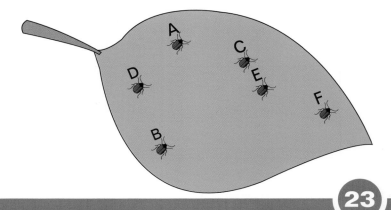

Unit 19: Time

Remember

When you are given a start time and a number of hours or minutes to work out the finish time, add the hours and then the minutes. Break up the minutes if you need to make it easier.

Example: A film starts at 7.40 and finishes 1 hour 30 minutes later. What time does the film end?

7.40 ➡ add 1 hour ➡ 8.40 ➡ add 20 minutes ➡ 9.00 ➡ add 10 minutes ➡ 9.10

Have a go

Draw the hands on the clock or write in the digital time for each start and finish time.

START		FINISH
	Sam goes shopping at 11.25 a.m. He gets home 2½ hours later.	
	A football match starts at 7.45 p.m. It finishes 90 minutes later.	
	A runner starts a marathon at 10.30 a.m. and finishes 3 hours 15 minutes later.	
	A plane takes off at 9.50 p.m. and lands 1 hour 45 minutes later.	
	Sophie starts washing the car at 2.25 p.m. and finishes 50 minutes later.	
	Daniel goes to the library at 4.40 p.m. and takes 35 minutes to choose some books.	

Remember

A bar chart shows information as a graph. Read the scale and labels on the **axes** carefully.

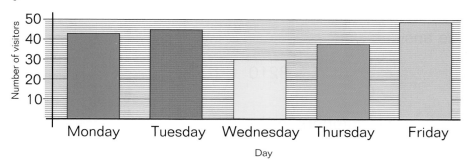

There were 49 visitors on Friday.

Have a go

This graph shows the average life-span of some different creatures.

Use the graph to answer these.

a What is the life-span of an African elephant? _____

b Which creature lives for 65 years? _____

c Which two creatures have the same average life-span?
_____ and _____

d For how many years on average does a cat live? _____

e Which creature lives half the number of years of an African elephant?

_____

f How many years longer does a human live than a cat? _____

g What is the difference in the life-spans of the dolphin and the trout? _____

h If a cat has 'nine lives', approximately how many years does each 'life' last?

_____

Check how much you have learned.

Answer the questions.
Mark your answers. Fill in your score.

SCORE

1 Write the answers.

a 395 × 10 ➡ ____

b 8210 ÷ 10 ➡ ____

out of 2

2 Write the missing numbers in these sequences.

a | −12 | | −2 | 3 | 8 | | |

b | 11 | 7 | | | −5 | | −13 |

out of 2

3 Measure these two lines.

a ____ mm

b ____ mm

c What is their difference in length? ____ mm

out of 3

4 This graph shows the heights of five children.

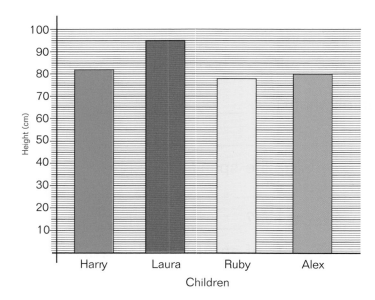

What is the difference in height between Laura and Alex? _____

out of 1

5 Answer these.

a 18 − (9 + 4) = _____

b (16 − 9) + (14 − 5) = _____

out of 2

6 Answer these.

a $\frac{1}{4}$ of 20 = _____

b $\frac{1}{3}$ of 12 = _____

c $\frac{1}{5}$ of 15 = _____

7 Join each shape to the correct part of this Venn diagram.

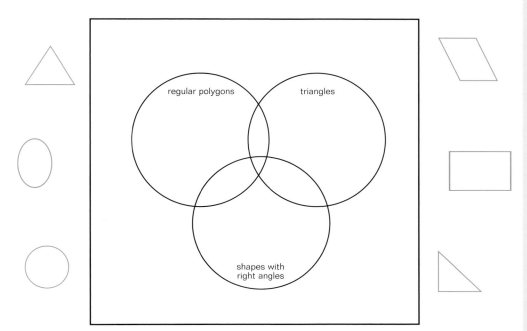

8 A tennis match starts at 4.50 p.m. and finishes 2 hours 15 minutes later. What time does the match end?

The match ends at _____.

9 Answer this.

$$\begin{array}{r} 869 \\ +378 \\ \hline \\ \hline \end{array}$$

10 Use your own written method to calculate the answer to this.

753 – 287

Test 2

Check how much you have learned.

Answer the questions.
Mark your answers. Fill in your score.

1 Look at the numbers below.

a Circle the multiples of 3.

b Tick the multiples of 4.

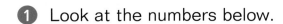

| 56 | 27 | 60 | 48 | 90 | 92 | 32 |

out of 2

2 Write the missing measures.

a $2\frac{1}{4}$ l = _____ ml

b 350 cm = _____ m

c $4\frac{3}{4}$ kg = _____ g

d 55 mm = _____ cm

out of 4

3 Answer these.

a 30 × 6 = _____

b 40 × 5 = _____

c 80 × 3 = _____

d 70 × 4 = _____

out of 4

4 Write the missing signs.

a (12 ☐ 9) ☐ 8 = 11

b 3 ☐ (9 ☐ 3) ☐ 5 = 23

out of 2

5

a Name this shape.

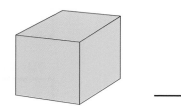

_____

b Write the number of faces, edges and vertices.

_____ faces _____ edges _____ vertices

out of 2

6 Put these angles in order of size, starting with the smallest.

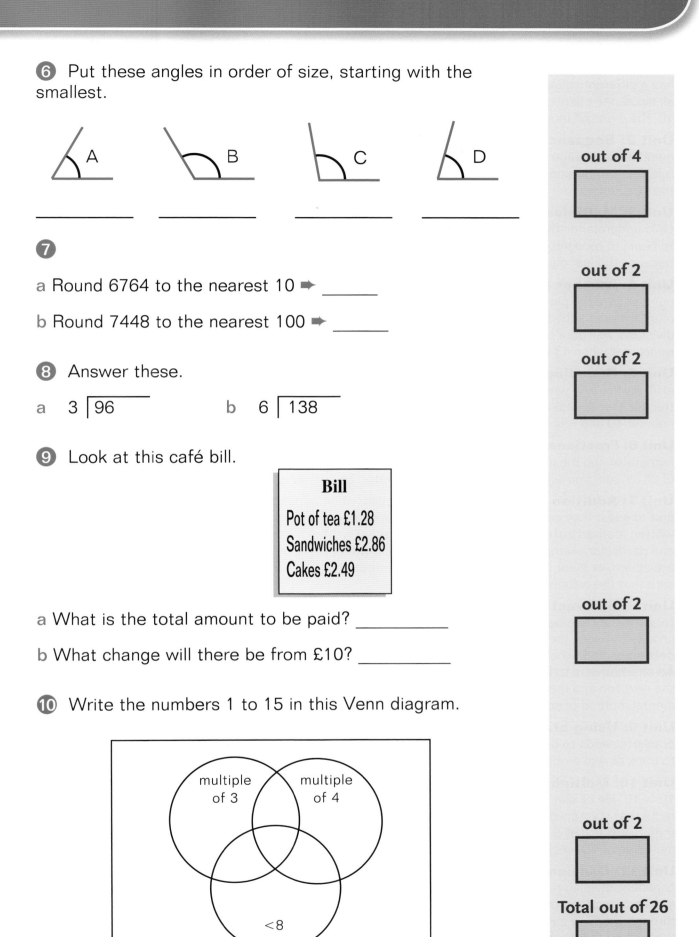

A   B   C   D

_____   _____   _____   _____

out of 4

7

a Round 6764 to the nearest 10 ➡ _____

b Round 7448 to the nearest 100 ➡ _____

out of 2

8 Answer these.

a   3 ⟌ 96   b   6 ⟌ 138

out of 2

9 Look at this café bill.

> **Bill**
>
> Pot of tea £1.28
> Sandwiches £2.86
> Cakes £2.49

a What is the total amount to be paid? _____

b What change will there be from £10? _____

out of 2

10 Write the numbers 1 to 15 in this Venn diagram.

multiple
of 3

multiple
of 4

<8

out of 2

Total out of 26

29

Parents' notes (Maths)

Unit 1: Place value   The place value is the position or place of a digit in a number. The same digit has a different value at different places in the number. When you multiply a number by 10, the digits all move one place to the left and a zero is put at the end of the number. When you divide a number by 10, the digits all move one place to the right and, if the number ends in zero, a zero is removed.

Unit 2: Sequences   Number sequences are lists of numbers with a pattern between each number. Encourage your child to work out the difference between each number, as that gives the rule for the missing numbers. If negative numbers are involved, make sure that zero is included in the sequences.

Unit 3: Multiples   Your child needs to recognise multiples of 2, 3, 4, 5 and 10. Make sure that your child understands that multiples don't stop at 10 $\times$ a number, but go on and on. The important thing is to begin to recognise the 'rule' for a set of multiples. For example, we know that 125 is a multiple of 5 because the last digit is a 5.

Unit 4: Number puzzles   Each of these maths puzzles is easier to solve if your child uses a set of number cards or pieces of paper with 1 to 20 written on them. These can be kept and used for other mental maths activities. For example, invite your child to lay the cards out and practise answering divisions. Ask your child to show the answer to 72 divided by 3, show 108 divided by 4, and show the remainder when 43 is divided by 9.

Unit 5: Rounding numbers   Being able to round numbers to the nearest 10 or 100 is a useful skill, particularly when trying to work out approximate answers to tricky calculations. Read through the rules for rounding, making sure that your child knows the difference between rounding to the nearest 10 and rounding to the nearest 100.

Unit 6: Fractions   Check that your child knows that the number above the line of a fraction is the numerator and the number below the line is the denominator. When the numerator is 1, to find a fraction of an amount you simply divide by the denominator. So $\frac{1}{5}$ of 20 is the same as $20 \div 5$, which is 4.

Unit 7: Addition   Always encourage your child, when adding two numbers, to look at the numbers first to see if they can be added mentally. If the numbers are too big, then your child will need to use a written method instead. There are several different written methods, and this 'vertical' method is just one particular example. It may be that your child wants to make informal jottings of numbers as they are added, or he or she may prefer the formal method shown. Go through each step carefully, making sure that the columns are lined up.

Unit 8: Subtraction   As with addition, always encourage your child to look at the numbers first to see if they can be subtracted mentally. If your child needs to use a written method he or she can choose between the two methods shown, or use his or her own method. The 'vertical' method is called decomposition, where tens and hundreds are exchanged to make the numbers easier to work with. An alternative is to find the difference between two numbers, counting on from the smaller number to the next ten and then on to the larger number. This is a good written method as it is the same as the mental method of counting on.

Unit 9: Using brackets   Brackets in a calculation show that the part of the calculation in the brackets needs to be worked out first. Compare calculations with brackets in different places and try to think of real problems that would need to be worked out in different orders.

Unit 10: Multiplication   Your child needs to learn all the multiplication tables facts up to 10 $\times$ 10. He or she should practise the facts and write down the ones that cause problems. Use the facts that your child knows to work out the others. For example, if your child knows that $8 \times 5 = 40$, then 8×6 is just 8 more. Your child can also use these facts to work out multiplications featuring multiples of 10, such as 80×5.

Unit 11: Division   Written division methods are quite tricky, so it is important that your child is confident dividing numbers mentally and knows the multiplication tables. This will help speed up the stages of working out a written division and allow your child to concentrate on the process. Read through the long method (where the number to be divided is broken up into tens and ones), and then relate this to the short method. The short method will be the one that your child will eventually use when carrying out written division calculations.

Unit 12: Mixed calculations Brackets in a calculation show that the part of the calculation in the brackets needs to be worked out first. To begin with, your child may need to write the answer to the part in the brackets above the calculation so that the rest of it can be worked out. With missing signs problems, your child may need to use trial-and-improvement methods, putting signs in to see if they work and then changing them for the correct answer.

Unit 13: Money calculations When adding money amounts that are difficult to do mentally, make sure that your child lines up the columns so that the decimal points are under each other. Then the normal written method for addition can be used. With subtraction or working out change it may be easier to use a 'shopkeeper's method', even as a written method. This involves counting on from the cost of the item to the amount given, writing down the money amounts as you go along and totalling the amount of change.

Unit 14: 2D shapes Polygons are two-dimensional shapes with straight sides. Each has a special name related to the number of sides, so, for example, any shape with five straight sides is a pentagon. A regular pentagon is one with equal length sides and equal angles. Make sure that your child understands the Venn diagram. The intersecting centre set is for a quadrilateral with right angles that is a regular polygon (a square), whereas the outside set (in the rectangle but outside the circles) is for non-regular polygons that do not have four sides and have no right angles.

Unit 15: 3D solids Your child will need to be able to recognise and name 3D solids and describe their properties. This will involve looking at the shapes of the faces and counting the number of faces, edges and vertices (corners). Prisms and pyramids can cause confusion. A pyramid has triangular sides that meet at a point. The base shape gives its name, e.g. 'square-based pyramid'. A prism has two end shapes that are identical, and rectangular sides. A triangular prism has two triangle end faces and three rectangle side faces.

Unit 16: Angles Ask your child to face in a certain direction and make turns clockwise and anticlockwise to specified angles, such as 90°, 45° or 180°. This can be related to a clock face. Your child needs to begin to get a feel for the size of different angles and be able to give an approximate measure in degrees.

Unit 17: Measures The metric system is a system of weights and measures. Your child should know that all the units in the metric system are in tens, hundreds and thousands, which makes it a lot easier to convert between measures than the old imperial system. Millimetres, metres, millilitres, litres, grams and kilograms are all examples of units in the metric system. Check that your child is able to convert fractions of quantities – at this stage only halves, quarters and tenths of centimetres, metres, litres or kilograms.

Unit 18: Length – millimetres Use a ruler to show your child how small a millimetre is. When measuring the lines and distances, make sure your child has the end of the ruler lined up exactly on one end point and uses the centimetre positions to help read the millimetres. When shopping in a DIY store, look out for lengths of wood etc. measured in millimetres.

Unit 19: Time When you are given a start time and the period of an event, it helps to picture a time line in your head to help you work out the finish time. Add on the hours first and then add on the minutes. Remind your child that there are 60 minutes in an hour. For example, if you go swimming at 3.40 for 1 hour 45 minutes, you will finish at 5.25: 3.40 → add 1 hour → 4.40 → add 20 minutes → 5.00 → add 25 minutes → 5.25. Answers for the digital clocks are given according to the 24-hour clock, which is correct for digital clocks. However, if your child has not yet learned the 24-hour clock, use of the 12-hour clock is acceptable.

Unit 20: Data – bar charts Bar charts or bar graphs are a very clear way of showing information as a graph. They can be horizontal or vertical in layout. Make sure that your child understands that the scale on each of these graphs has only the tens numbered. It is important to read all the information about each graph, such as title and axis headings, so that your child has a good understanding of the graph.

Answers (Maths)

Unit 1: Place value (page 6)

1 a 890   b 760   c 310   d 920
e 600   f 3140   g 2960   h 4880
i 7200   j 8970

2 a 62   b 81   c 20   d 47
e 99   f 184   g 309   h 766
i 850   j 687

3 a 756   7560   7460   746   747
b 3970   4070   4060   4160   416
c 1080   1090   109   99   990

4 Check the calculations on your child's own chain.

Unit 2: Sequences (page 7)

1 a 8   13   18   23   Rule: + 5
b −1   1   3   5   Rule: + 2
c 0   3   6   9   Rule: + 3
d −2   −6   −10   −14   Rule: − 4
e 10   0   −10   −20   Rule: − 10
f −1   −6   −11   −16   Rule: − 5

2 a −2   4   16
b 33   3   −7
c −6   −2   4
d −2   4   7

Unit 3: Multiples (page 8)

1 multiples of 3:   75   54   30   48
60   27   120   90   45
multiples of 4:   68   40   48   60
52   120   100
multiples of 5:   75   40   30   85
60   120   90   100   45
multiples of 3,4 and 5:   60   120

2 a Numbers coloured will make a diagonal pattern (in SE direction starting on
3, 6, 9, 12, 15, 18, 21 and 81.
b Numbers circled should be in columns down starting with the numbers   4, 8, 12, 16, 20.

Unit 4: Number puzzles (page 9)

1 There are many possible solutions.

2

	multiple of 3	not a multiple of 3
even number	6 > 10 12, 18	2, 4, 8, 10 14, 16, 20
	15	11, 13, 17, 19
not an even number	3, 9	1, 5, 7

Unit 5: Rounding numbers (page 10)

1 a 760   b 380   c 150   d 210
e 740   f 940   g 1570   h 6380
i 8930   j 3050   k 7950   l 2330

2 a 500   b 300   c 100   d 700
e 600   f 900   g 6900   h 1800
i 8700   j 2200   k 3400   l 2700

3 a 520   320   1200
b 5400   4500   200 000

Unit 6: Fractions (page 11)

1 a 3   b 5   c 4   d 4   e 1   f 3

2 a 4   3   7   6   5
b 2   5   6   8   7
c 6   10   7   5   9
d 5   2   7   6   9

Unit 7: Addition (page 12)

1 a 632   b 721   c 911   d 745
e 1051   f 1165   g 1327   h 1480

2 a 5̲61   7̲2̲8   b 8̲7̲6
c 3̲57   6̲1̲8̲   d   20̲4̲   6̲9̲3

Unit 8: Subtraction (page 13)

1 a 617   b 271   c 149   d 278
e 269   f 419

2 a 209   b 351   c 151   d 154
e 144   f 417

Unit 9: Using brackets (page 14)

1 a 4   b 5   c 12   d 4
e 4   f 20   g 15   h 16

2 a 10   b 1   c 9   d 2   e 26   f 13

3 a $14-8+18$ b $32-6-2$
c $17+19-12$ d $13+5+6$
e $31-12+5$ f $8-5+21$

Unit 10: Multiplication (page 15)

1
a 24   48   18   21   32
b 35   36   28   81   49
c 24   56   72   16   80
d 27   50   20   42   54

2
a 350   150   450   200   300
b 300   240   480   360   180
c 140   350   560   280   490
d 320   160   480   720   400

Unit 11: Division (page 16)

1
a 25   b 14   c 23   d 29   e 16
f 16   g 34   h 13   i 27   j 15

1
a 17 r2   b 24   c 16 r3
   5)87   4)96   4)67
d 16   e 12 r2
   6)96   7)86

Unit 12: Mixed calculations (page 17)

1
a $\times$ $+$ b $-$ $+$ c $-$ $+$
d $\times$ $-$ e $\times$ $+$ f $\div$ $+$

2
a $\times$ $+$ b $+$ $-$ c $\times$ $\div$
d $\times$ $+$ $\times$ e $+$ $-$ $\times$ f $+$ $\times$ $-$

Unit 13: Money calculations (page 18)

a cost: £8.91   change: £11.09
b cost: £8.94   change: £11.06
c cost: £8.85   change: £11.15
d cost: £9.96   change: £10.04
e cost: £8.67   change: £11.33
f cost: £9.42   change: £10.58

Unit 14: 2D shapes (page 19)

1
a hexagon
b square or quadrilateral
c triangle   d octagon
e triangle   f pentagon

g heptagon   h kite or quadrilateral
i quadrilateral or parallelogram
j circle   k semicircle   l oval

2
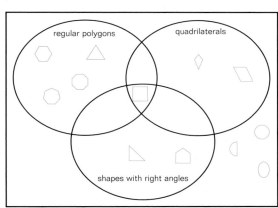

Unit 15: 3D solids (page 20)

1
a pyramid
5 faces   8 edges   5 vertices
b cuboid
6 faces   12 edges   8 vertices
c pyramid or tetrahedron
4 faces   6 edges   4 vertices
d prism
5 faces   9 edges   6 vertices

2
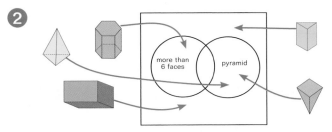

Unit 16: Angles (page 21)

1
a B, D, A, C   b B, D, A, C
c A, B, C, D   d B, D, A, C
e D, B, C, A

2

Time	Clockwise angle of turn	New time
3 o'clock	90°	6 o'clock
1 o'clock	180°	7 o'clock
6 o'clock	90°	9 o'clock
10 o'clock	360°	10 o'clock
5 o'clock	90°	8 o'clock
7 o'clock	90°	10 o'clock
5 o'clock	180°	11 o'clock

Unit 17: Measures (page 22)

1 a $2\frac{1}{2}$ km   b 6000 m   c $2\frac{1}{2}$ m
d $4\frac{1}{2}$ cm   e 12 km   f $20\frac{1}{2}$ m
g 140 mm   h 11 000 m   i 200 cm

2 a 4 kg   b 3500 g   c $1\frac{1}{4}$ kg
d 10 000 g   e $6\frac{1}{2}$ kg   f 5250 g
g $3\frac{3}{4}$ kg   h 2750 g   i $4\frac{1}{2}$ kg

3 a 4 l   b 8000 ml   c $1\frac{1}{2}$ l
d 2750 ml   e $4\frac{1}{4}$ l   f 12 000 ml
g $4\frac{3}{4}$ l   h 4250 ml   i 2500 ml

Unit 18: Length – millimetres (page 23)

1 a 40 mm   b 25 mm   c 65 mm
d 30 mm   e 55 mm   f 70 mm
g 35 mm   h 45 mm

2 a F   b E   c C   d B   e E

Unit 19: Time (page 24)

START		FINISH
11.25 a.m.	Sam goes shopping at 11.25a.m. He gets home $2\frac{1}{2}$ hours later.	1.55
19:45	A football match starts at 7.45p.m. It finishes 90 minutes later.	21:15
10.30	A runner starts a marathon at 10.30a.m. and finishes 3 hours 15 minutes later.	1.45
21:50	A plane takes off at 9.50p.m. and lands 1 hour 45 minutes later.	23:35
2.25	Sophie starts washing the car at 2.25p.m. and finishes 50 minutes later.	3.15
16:40	Daniel goes to the library at 4.40p.m. and takes 35 minutes to choose some books.	17:15

Unit 20: Data – bar charts (page 25)

a 60 years   b dolphin
c human and raven   d 18 years
e horse   f 52 years longer
g 55 years   h 2 years

Test 1 (pages 26 and 27)

1 a 3950   b 821

2 a   −7   13   18
b   3   −1   −9

3 a 25 mm   b 40 mm   c 15 mm

4 a 15 cm

5 a 5   b 16

6 a 5   b 4   c 3

7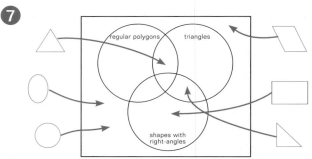

8 7.05 p.m.

9 1247

10 466

Test 2 (pages 28 and 29)

1 a and b

56   (27)   (60)   (48)   (90)   92   32

2 a 2250 ml   b $3\frac{1}{2}$ m   c 4750 g
d $5\frac{1}{2}$ cm

3 a 180   b 200   c 240   d 280

4 a − +   b × − +

5 a cube
b 6 faces   12 edges   8 vertices

6 A, D, C, B

7 a 6760   b 7400

8 a 32   b 23

9 a £6.63   b £3.37

10

13	multiple of 3: 9, 15	multiple of 4: 8	14
	12		
	3, 6	4	
11	<8 : 1, 2, 5, 7		10

Remember

Homophones are words that **sound alike** but have **different spellings** or **meanings**.

"Come out of the **sun**," the woman said to her **son**.

Have a go

Rewrite each sentence. Use the correct homophone in place of the underlined word.

a The postman pushed the <u>male</u> through the letter box.

_____

b There is a <u>whole</u> in my sock.

_____

c There was a dirty mark on the <u>sealing</u>.

_____

d A loud <u>grown</u> came from behind the door.

_____

e The <u>missed</u> rose from the marshes.

_____

f Have you <u>herd</u> any good jokes?

_____

g The train roared <u>threw</u> the tunnel.

_____

h You must have <u>patients</u> when you are waiting for a bus.

_____

i I ate a big <u>peace</u> of the cake.

_____

j We took the shortest <u>root</u> to London.

_____

k The girl had <u>fare</u> hair.

_____

l The <u>night</u> wore a suit of armour.

_____

Unit 2: Revising verb tenses

 Remember

The **tense** of a verb tells us **when** an action took place.

Yesterday I **swam** in the pool.

This happened in the **past**. It is in the **past tense**.

Now I **am swimming** in the sea.

This is happening **now**. It is in the **present tense**.

Tomorrow I **will swim** in the river.

This will happen in the **future**. It is in the **future tense**.

 **Have a go**

1 Complete this chart.

verb	present tense	future tense
wait	I am waiting	I **will wait** _____
walk	You are walking	You **will** _____
hop	He is hopping	He _____
shout	She is shouting	She _____
come	It is coming	It _____
act	We are acting	We _____
laugh	You are laughing	You _____
skip	They are skipping	They _____

2 Rewrite each sentence in the future tense.

a I got up early. ⟶ <u>I will get up early.</u>

b I ate my breakfast. ⟶ _____

c I watched TV for half an hour. ⟶ _____

d Then I read my book. ⟶ _____

e At nine o'clock I called for my friend. ⟶ _____

f We walked to the park. ⟶ _____

g We played on the swings for a while. ⟶ _____

h Then we had an ice cream. ⟶ _____

Unit 3: Letter patterns – *dge*

Remember

Always look carefully at words to see if you can spot any common **letter patterns**.

a he**dge**

a bri**dge**

Have a go

1 Choose the correct vowel to complete each word. Read the words you make.

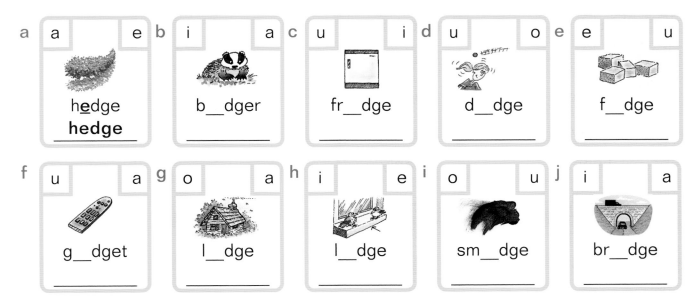

a	a / e	b	i / a	c	u / i	d	u / o	e	e / u

a | h_e_dge | **hedge**

b | b__dger | _____

c | fr__dge | _____

d | d__dge | _____

e | f__dge | _____

f | u / a — g__dget | _____

g | o / a — l__dge | _____

h | i / e — l__dge | _____

i | o / u — sm__dge | _____

j | i / a — br__dge | _____

2 Complete the chart with the words you made.

adge words	edge words	idge words	odge words	udge words

3 Try this letter pattern challenge. Think of as many other words containing each letter pattern as possible. Add the words to the correct column of the chart.

Scoring

0-5 words - fair	6-10 words - good	11-15 words - very good	16-20 words - excellent

Unit 4: Revising adverbs

⬤ Remember

An **adverb** tells us more about a **verb**.
Adverbs often tell us **how** something happened.
Many adverbs end in **ly**.

Tara smiled **happily** when she opened her present.

⬤ Have a go

1 Match up the pairs of adverbs with similar meanings.

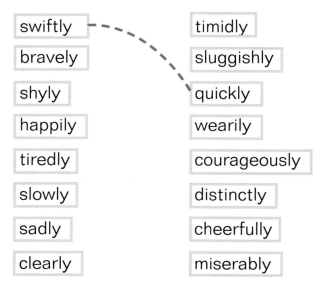

swiftly	timidly
bravely	sluggishly
shyly	quickly
happily	wearily
tiredly	courageously
slowly	distinctly
sadly	cheerfully
clearly	miserably

2 Change the adverb in each sentence to make it mean the opposite.

a I sighed <u>happily</u>. _____

b The children spoke <u>noisily</u>. _____

c I put my clothes <u>tidily</u> on the chair. _____

d I did all my sums <u>incorrectly</u>. _____

e The nurse treated me <u>gently</u>. _____

f The river flowed <u>rapidly</u>. _____

g The boy spoke <u>politely</u>. _____

h I did my writing <u>carelessly</u>. _____

Unit 5: Revising syllables

Remember

When you say longer words **slowly** you can hear how they can be **broken down into smaller parts**. These parts are called **syllables**.

la – bel    ro – bot   spi – der

When you say the words above, the **emphasis** (or stress) is on the **first** syllable which contains a **long** vowel (the **vowel** says its name).
When you split the word, you split it after the long vowel.

Have a go

1 Do these syllable sums.

a po + em = _____   b la + zy = _____

c stu + dent = _____   d la + bel = _____

e ro + bot = _____   f pa + per = _____

g ti + dy = _____   h stu + pid = _____

i e + vil = _____   j re + cent = _____

2 Write the words you made.

First syllable ends with a long:				
a	e	i	o	u
lazy				

3 Split these words into two syllables.

a pupil = __pu + pil__   b silent = _____

c acorn = _____   d open = _____

e diet = _____   f gravy = _____

g later = _____   h pony = _____

i duty = _____   j tiger = _____

Unit 6: Nouns – diminutives

A **noun** is a **naming** word. The **diminutive** form of a noun
is a **smaller** form of a thing or person.

a duck and a duckling
(**Duckling** is the **diminutive** form of **duck**.)

Have a go

Match up each animal with its young.

Write them here.

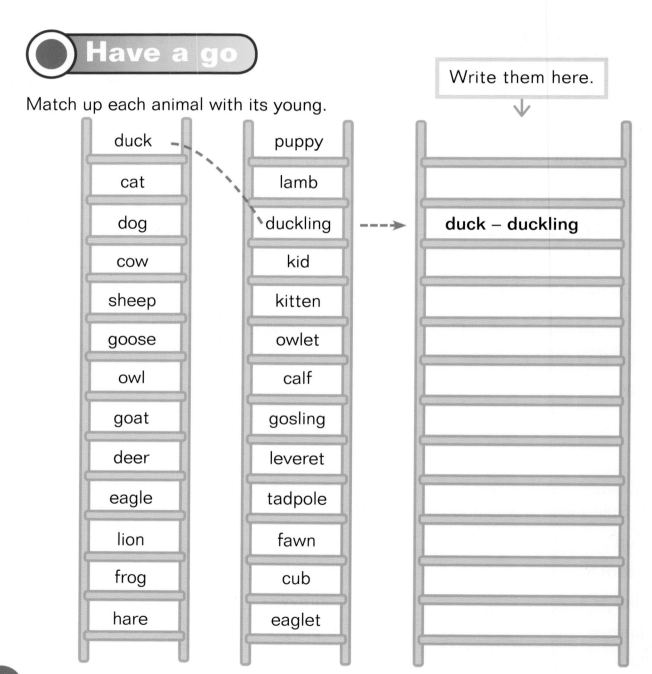

duck	puppy	
cat	lamb	**duck – duckling**
dog	duckling	
cow	kid	
sheep	kitten	
goose	owlet	
owl	calf	
goat	gosling	
deer	leveret	
eagle	tadpole	
lion	fawn	
frog	cub	
hare	eaglet	

Unit 7: Confusing words

Remember

Do not **confuse** words which **sound** the **same** but have **different meanings**.

I have **two** sweets.

We use **two** as a number word.

I am going **to** the shop.

We use **to** as a preposition.

I am going **to** play cricket.

We use **to** as part of a verb.

May I have a cake **too**?

We use **too** to mean as well.

It is **too** cold!

We use **too** to mean extremely.

Have a go

1 Fill in each gap with **two** or **too**.

a It will take me _____ seconds.

b It is _____ hard for me to do.

c I would like an ice cream _____.

d I have written _____ letters.

e May I come _____?

f The tree was _____ high to climb.

g It is _____ late to go out.

h You wear _____ socks.

i I have _____ pets.

j I feel _____ hot in the sun.

2 Fill in each gap with **to** or **too**.

a I want _____ play the piano.

b I want to learn to play it _____.

c Is it _____ difficult?

d You must go ___ a piano teacher ___ learn.

3 Fill in each gap with **two**, **to** or **too**.

The _____ men tried _____ climb the mountain but it was _____ high.

41

Unit 8: Similes

Remember

A **simile** helps us to **describe** things better.
It **compares two things**.
Many similes contain **adjectives**.

The box looked heavy but it was **as light as a feather**.

Have a go

1 Choose an adjective from the box to complete these similes about animals.

| heavy | slow | sly | busy | slippery | hairy | playful | strong |

a   as <u>**sly**</u> as a fox

b   as _____ as a tortoise

c   as _____ as an eel

d   as _____ as a kitten

e   as _____ as an elephant

f   as _____ as an ox

g   as _____ as a bee

h   as _____ as a gorilla

| red | sharp | graceful | sweet | flat | dry | smooth | cool |

2 Choose an adjective from the box to complete each of these similes.

a   as _____ as honey

b   as _____ as silk

c   as _____ as a razor

d   as _____ as a pancake

e   as _____ as a cucumber

f   as _____ as beetroot

g   as _____ as a swan

h   as _____ as dust

Unit 9: Prefixes – *in, im, il* and *ir*

A **prefix** is a **group of letters** we add to the **beginning** of a word.
Prefixes change the **meaning** of a word.
If you add the prefixes **in**, **im**, **il** or **ir** to words it often gives them the **opposite** meaning.

patient

impatient

Have a go

1 Do these prefix sums. Read the words you make.

a in + capable = <u>incapable</u>

b ir + responsible = _____

c im + mature = _____

d il + legible = _____

e il + legal = _____

f ir + regular = _____

g im + perfect = _____

h im + patient = _____

i in + adequate = _____

j in + considerate = _____

2 Write the opposite of:

a legal _____

b legible _____

c regular _____

d responsible _____

e capable _____

f adequate _____

g considerate _____

h mature _____

i patient _____

j perfect _____

3 Add the prefix **il**, **im**, **in** or **ir** to give each word the opposite meaning.
Use a dictionary if necessary.

a ___ logical

b ___ appropriate

c ___ practical

d ___ resistible

e ___ competent

f ___ accurate

g ___ pertinent

h ___ literate

i ___ rational

j ___ curable

k ___ visible

l ___ proper

Unit 10: Writing sensible sentences

● Remember

A sentence should always **make sense** and be **accurate**.

The boy were hurt. ✗   The boy was hurt. ✓

● Have a go

1 Complete each sentence with '**was**' or '**were**'.

a The boys _____ playing football.

b Some children _____ very noisy.

c The dog _____ hungry.

d What _____ you looking for?

e I _____ climbing the tree when I fell.

f They _____ getting ready to go out.

g He _____ going to a party.

h Who _____ you talking to?

2 Rewrite the following sentences correctly.

a The apples what we ate was sweet.

_____

b The children was very naughty.

_____

c "I haven't done nothing wrong!" the thief protested.

_____

d The child did not take no notice of her teacher.

_____

e Pass me them books, please.

_____

f The instructor learned the woman how to drive.

_____

g The girl throwed her rubbish in the bin.

_____

h I done 20 sums this morning.

_____

Unit 11: Tricky spellings

 Remember

When the letter **g** is **followed** by **e i** or **y** we often put **u** after it, to help it keep its hard sound.

gitar ☒      **gu**itar ☑

 **Have a go**

1 Fill in the missing **u** in each word. Read the words you make.

a g __ y   b rog __ e   c vag __ e   d g __ itar   e g __ ess

f g __ ide   g g __ ilty   h plag __ e   i leag __ e   j catalog __ e

2 Write the words that:

| begin with **gu** | _____ | _____ | _____ | _____ | _____ |
| end with **gue** | _____ | _____ | _____ | _____ | _____ |

3 Write the word from question 1 that means:

a _____ not clear

b _____ not innocent

c _____ a stringed instrument

d _____ a man

e _____ a deadly disease

f _____ a leader

g _____ an estimate

h _____ a rascal

i _____ a complete list

j _____ a group of sports teams

4 Write these **gu** words in alphabetical order:

| tongue | guard | fatigue | dialogue |
| intrigue | guest | disguise | guarantee |

a _____   b _____   c _____   d _____

e _____   f _____   g _____   h _____

Unit 12: Revising pronouns

Remember

A **pronoun** is a word that **takes the place of a noun**.

I rode with **him**.

A pronoun is **singular** when it stands for **one** person or thing.

When the children went out, **they** rode with **us**.

A pronoun is **plural** when it stands for **more than one** person or thing.

Have a go

1 Say if the underlined pronoun is singular (**S**) or plural (**P**).

a I (**S**) can run fast.

b He (__) looked out of the window.

c They (__) had something to eat.

d We (__) did painting at school today.

e "Can you (__) help?" Sam asked Ben.

f When the car came round the corner it (__) crashed.

g The cat chased the birds but did not catch them (__).

h When she (__) got home, Beth watched television.

2 Find the pronouns hiding in the puzzle.

Write each pronoun here.
Say if it is singular or plural.

__me (singular)__

a	b	c	d	m	e	f	g
h	i	j	k	l	s	h	e
m	n	p	v	i	t	w	x
t	h	e	y	z	x	c	v
c	d	e	h	i	m	f	h
i	j	o	u	r	m	n	b
q	w	t	h	e	m	x	r
b	v	c	h	e	r	x	z

_____

_____

_____

_____

_____

_____

Remember

We use **speech marks** when we write down what people say.

"What's the matter?" Meg asked. Suki replied, "I feel ill!"

When we are writing a **script for a play**, we set out speech a little differently.

Meg: What's the matter?
Suki: I feel ill!

Have a go

Rewrite this conversation as a playscript.

"What's the matter, Tom?" the teacher asked.
Tom replied, "I am having trouble with my picture."
"How can I help you?" the teacher enquired.
Tom said, "I can't seem to find the right green for this tree."
"Have you tried mixing up some paints?" the teacher asked.
Tom replied, "Which colours do I mix to make green?"
"Try using some blue and yellow paint," the teacher answered.
Tom exclaimed, "Look! That's much better!"
"Well done!" the teacher smiled.

Teacher: <u>**What's the matter, Tom?**</u>

Tom: _____

Teacher: _____

Tom: _____

Teacher: _____

Tom: _____

Teacher: _____

Tom: _____

Teacher: _____

Remember

Some **nouns** (naming words) and **adjectives** (describing words) end with **ar**.

The burgl**ar** was very muscul**ar**.
(noun)   (adjective)

Have a go

1 Match up the **ar** nouns with their meanings.

beggar	someone who breaks into houses to steal
grammar	a sour liquid
cellar	someone who begs
burglar	someone who is in charge of a church
sugar	the rules of our language
vinegar	someone who studies at school
collar	a room underneath a house
vicar	a substance put in foods or drinks to sweeten them
scholar	a post that helps to hold up a building
pillar	the part of a shirt that goes round the neck

2 Circle the **ar** adjectives.   Write them here.

q	w	r	e	g	u	l	a	r	t	y	u
z	x	c	v	f	a	m	i	l	i	a	r
l	p	a	r	t	i	c	u	l	a	r	m
b	v	c	p	o	p	u	l	a	r	j	h
d	r	m	u	s	c	u	l	a	r	f	g
a	s	d	f	g	s	i	m	i	l	a	r
c	i	r	c	u	l	a	r	w	r	t	f

regular _____

_____

_____

_____

_____

_____

Unit 15: Revising prepositions

Remember

Prepositions tell us **where** something or someone is.
A preposition often tells us about the **position** of something or someone.

The snake is **behind** the rock.

Have a go

1 Find and circle a preposition in each word.

a th(under)	b supply	c snatch	d coffee
e hover	f only	g pastry	h window

2 Use the prepositions you found to complete these sentences:

a I put some water _____ the kettle.

b Tom laughed _____ the funny clown.

c The child hid _____ the bed.

d I fell _____ my bike.

e The fast car zoomed _____ the slow old car.

f The lift went _____ to the next floor.

g The girl is sitting _____ the chair.

h The helicopter flew _____ the wood.

Remember

Some words contain the **same letter patterns**, but they are **pronounced differently**.

vase

case

Have a go

1 Make these words. One has been done for you.

ough

b**ough**   t_____   c_____   r_____
bough   _____   _____   _____

ough

thr_____   tr_____   th_____   en_____
_____   _____   _____   _____

ough

n_____t   f_____t   b_____t   br_____t
_____   _____   _____   _____

2 Sort the words into sets according to the way the **ough** is pronounced.

Rhymes with:					
port	stuff	zoo	toe	how	scoff
nought					

Unit 17: Joining sentences

The **two** sentences below have been written as **one** sentence by **missing out some words** and by changing the word order. Notice that the **meaning** still remains the **same**.

The man was angry. He shouted at the motorist.
The angry man shouted at the motorist.

1 Make each pair of sentences into one sentence.

a The boy was hungry. He asked for a sandwich.

   The hungry boy asked for a sandwich.

b The man was kind. He helped the old woman.

_____

c The woman was brave. She rescued the drowning child.

_____

d The builder was busy. He was laying some bricks.

_____

e The car is old. It should not be on the road.

_____

f The woman is young. She is wearing a lovely dress.

_____

g The windows are dirty. They need cleaning.

_____

h The case was light. It was easy to pick up.

_____

i The boy was tired. He could not run any further.

_____

j The castle was old. It stood on top of the hill.

_____

Unit 18: Suffixes – *ness, hood, ship*

Remember

A **suffix** is a **group of letters** we can add to the **end** of a word.
Suffixes **change** the **meanings** of words.

sick
(root word)

sick**ness**
(+ suffix **ness**)

Have a go

1 Choose either the suffix **ness**, **hood** or **ship** to add to each word.

a	ill**ness**	b	child_____	c	dark_____	d	friend_____
e	boy_____	f	parent_____	g	bright_____	h	leader____
i	sick_____	j	sad_____	k	neighbour_____	l	scholar_____
m	blind_____	n	girl_____	o	hard_____	p	quiet_____
q	man_____	r	fellow_____	s	adult_____	t	good_____

2 Write the words you made in the correct columns.

-ness words	-hood words	-ship words

Unit 19: Apostrophes

Remember

We can **shorten** some words by missing some letters out.
We put an **apostrophe** to show where letters are missing.

Who's got some money?

I've got some.

who's = who has

I've = I have

Have a go

1 Put in the missing apostrophes.

a cant	b didnt	c Im	d youll	e theyre
f thats	g dont	h couldnt	i hadnt	j hes

2 Copy each sentence. Write the longer form of the shortened words.

a The letter hasn't come yet. _____

b I won't do it again. _____

c You shouldn't run across a busy road. _____

d That's my coat on the hook. _____

e There's no-one at home. _____

f How's your bad leg? _____

g We're going out soon. _____

h You've got a lovely smile. _____

Unit 20: Using a dictionary

Remember

A dictionary may be used to help you spell difficult words.

dynosaur   dinosawr   dienosore   dinosaur

Have a go

There is something wrong with each of the 20 words below.
Look the words up in a dictionary. Write each word correctly.

a	clowd	_____	b	stedy	_____
c	scrach	_____	d	gardner	_____
e	intresting	_____	f	airoplane	_____
g	swiming	_____	h	writeing	_____
i	joyned	_____	j	noisey	_____
k	frightend	_____	l	awkword	_____
m	cuboard	_____	n	sqware	_____
o	befor	_____	p	tresher	_____
q	carefull	_____	r	allways	_____
s	shood	_____	t	lorrys	_____

Test 1

Check how much you have learned.

Answer the questions.
Mark your answers. Fill in your score.

1 Replace the word in brackets with the correct word.

a The robber tried to (steel) _____ my watch.

b I ate a (current) _____ bun.

2 Rewrite the verb in brackets in the future tense.

a I (rode) _____ my bike to the park.

b I (went) _____ on the slide.

3 Fill in the missing letters in each word.

a

bri_____

b

sle_____

4 Write an adverb that means the opposite of each of these:

a quickly _____   b tidily _____

5 Split each word into two syllables.

a robot = _____ + _____

b tiger = _____ + _____

6 Choose the correct word to complete each sentence.

duckling	gosling

a A young goose is called a _____.

b A young duck is called a _____.

7 Choose **to**, **too** or **two** to complete each sentence.

a It is _____ far to walk.

b I am going _____ the library.

8 Complete each simile with the best adjective.

fast   **slow**

a as _____ as a snail

b as _____ as a cheetah

9 Choose the correct prefix to begin each word.

a

im	in

____ possible

b

il	ir

____ regular

10 Choose **was** or **were** to complete each sentence.

a We _____ late home.

b I _____ reading a book.

Test 2

Check how much you have learned.

Answer the questions.
Mark your answers. Fill in your score.

1 Fill in the missing letters.

a

g___ide

b

tong___

out of 2

2 Say if each pronoun is singular (**S**) or plural (**P**).

a They (_____) were shouting.

b She (___) bought a loaf.

out of 2

3 Rewrite this conversation like a playscript.

"Why are you unhappy?" Anna asked.

The dragon replied, "My fire has gone out!"

Anna: _____

Dragon: _____

out of 2

4 Choose **or**, **er** or **ar** to complete each word.

a vineg_____   b sug_____

out of 2

5 Underline the preposition in each town's name.

| Dover | Sunderland |

out of 2

6 Fill in the missing letters.

a

c_____

b

pl_____

7 Rewrite each pair of sentences as one sentence.

a The woman was tired. She went to bed.

_____

b The toy was broken. It was on the floor.

_____

8 Choose the suffix **ness**, **hood** or **ship** to complete each word.

a | friend _____

b | bright _____

9 Put in the missing apostrophe marks.

a theyre

b dont

10 Spell each word correctly. Use a dictionary if necessary.

a suddenley

b scard

Parents' notes (English)

Unit 1: Revising homophones Words that sound the same but have different meanings are called homophones. ('Homo' means 'the same' and 'phone' means 'sound'.) Encourage your child to use a dictionary to check the correct spelling if in doubt.

Unit 2: Revising verb tenses When a verb tells of an action taking place now, we say that it is written in the present tense. A verb describing an action which has already taken place is written in the past tense. (For example, "Last week I bought a new car.") A verb describing something that will happen in the future is written in the future tense. ("Tomorrow I will go to town.")

Unit 3: Letter patterns – *dge* There are many common letter patterns (letters which frequently come together) in words. It is important for your child to recognise these when reading and to be able to use them when writing. The letter pattern **dge** is the focus of this unit.

Unit 4: Revising adverbs Remind your child that an adverb tells us more about a verb. Many adverbs (adverbs of manner) tell us about how something happened. These adverbs often end with the suffix **ly**.

Unit 5: Revising syllables When we say words slowly we can hear how they may be broken down into smaller parts, called syllables. It is helpful to tap or clap these 'beats' when saying words in order to stress the syllables. When we say words in which the **emphasis** (or stress) is on the **first** syllable which contains a **long vowel** (vowel that says its name) the first syllable is always left **open** (ending with the vowel) e.g. ro – bot.

Unit 6: Nouns – diminutives Nouns (naming words) that imply something small, like animal young, are called diminutives. Sometimes a diminutive may be made by adding a suffix (e.g. duck – duckling). Sometimes the diminutive is unlike the larger form (e.g. dog – puppy).

Unit 7: Confusing words There are many words which sound alike, but which have different functions that sometimes confuse children. In this activity the words **two** (when referring to a number), **to** (when used as a preposition, e.g. "I went to the shop." or as part of a verb e.g. "I like to sing.") and **too** (meaning 'as well' e.g. "I'll have some too." or meaning 'extremely' e.g. "It was too hard.") are focused on.

Unit 8: Similes Remind your child that an adjective is a describing word. It tells us more about a noun. Adjectives help make writing more interesting and descriptive. Similes often use adjectives to compare two things.

Unit 9: Prefixes – *in, im, il* and *ir* Remind your child that a prefix is a group of letters we can add to the front of a word. Prefixes change the meaning of the word. The addition of the prefixes **in**, **im**, **il** and **ir** often give words the opposite meaning.

Unit 10: Writing sensible sentences A sentence is basically a unit of meaning and should make sense. This unit asks your child to compose grammatically correct sentences. It is important to get your child to check sentences he or she has written to make sure no silly errors have been made.

Unit 11: Tricky spellings It is helpful to provide your child with simple rules to help him or her understand the spelling of some tricky words. When the letter **g** is followed by **e**, **i** or **y** we often put **u** after it, to help it keep its hard sound.

Unit 12: Revising pronouns Remind your child that a pronoun is a word that takes the place of a noun. ('Pro' actually means 'in place of'.) Pronouns may be singular (when they stand for one person or thing) or plural (when they stand for more than one person or thing).

Unit 13: Revising speech marks When we write down what people say, we use speech marks. The words a person says should go inside the speech marks. This unit shows how the same dialogue (piece of speech using speech marks) may be set out as a playscript.

Unit 14: Common word endings – *ar* There are many common word endings. It is important for your child to recognise these when reading and to be able to use them when writing. The common word ending **ar** is the focus of this unit. Many nouns (naming words) and adjectives (describing words) end with **ar**.

Unit 15: Revising prepositions Remind your child that prepositions often tell us about the position of one thing in relation to another e.g. The train went <u>through</u> the tunnel.

Unit 16: Letter patterns and sounds Words often contain common letter patterns, which, while they may look the same, do not sound the same. The context in which a word is used provides the clue as to how the word should be pronounced. The **ough** letter pattern, which can be pronounced in many different ways, is the focus of this unit.

Unit 17: Joining sentences The activities in this unit show how pairs of sentences may be written as one sentence by missing out some words and changing the order of words whilst retaining the same meaning.

Unit 18: Suffixes – *ness, hood, ship* A suffix is a group of letters we add to the end of a word. Your child needs to understand that many words may be extended by adding suffixes. Adding a suffix changes the meaning of the word in some way. In this unit it is shown how some words may be suffixed by adding **ness**, **hood** and **ship** to the end of them.

Unit 19: Apostrophes We sometimes shorten words and miss out letters. These words are called contractions. (To 'contract' means to make shorter.) We use an apostrophe to show where letters are missing.

Unit 20: Using a dictionary A dictionary is a very valuable tool. Your child needs to know how to use one. This unit focuses on its function as an aid to spelling.

Answers (English)

Unit 1: Revising homophones (page 35)

a The postman pushed the <u>mail</u> through the letter box.

b There is a <u>hole</u> in my sock.

c There was a dirty mark on the <u>ceiling</u>.

d A loud <u>groan</u> came from behind the door.

e The <u>mist</u> rose from the marshes.

f Have you <u>heard</u> any good jokes?

g The train roared <u>through</u> the tunnel.

h You must have <u>patience</u> when you are waiting for a bus.

i I ate a big <u>piece</u> of the cake.

j We took the shortest <u>route</u> to London.

k The girl had <u>fair</u> hair.

l The <u>knight</u> wore a suit of armour.

Unit 2: Revising verb tenses (page 36)

1

verb	present tense	future tense
wait	I am waiting	I will wait
walk	You are walking	You will walk
hop	He is hopping	He will hop
shout	She is shouting	She will shout
come	It is coming	It will come
act	We are acting	We will act
laugh	You are laughing	You will laugh
skip	They are skipping	They will skip

2
a I will get up early.

b I will eat my breakfast.

c I will watch TV for half an hour.

d Then I will read my book.

e At nine o'clock I will call for my friend.

f We will walk to the park.

g We will play on the swings for a while.

h Then we will have an ice cream.

Unit 3: Letter patterns – *dge* (page 37)

1
a hedge   b badger   c fridge
d dodge   e fudge   f gadget
g lodge   h ledge   i smudge
j bridge

2

adge words	edge words	idge words	odge words	udge words
badger	hedge	fridge	dodge	fudge
gadget	ledge	bridge	lodge	smudge

3 The answers below are examples only.

adge words	edge words	idge words	odge words	udge words
cadge	edge	fidget	bodge	judge
badge	wedge	midge	codger	nudge
	dredge	midget	stodge	sludge
		ridge	lodger	trudge

Unit 4: Revising adverbs (page 38)

1

swiftly	timidly
bravely	sluggishly
shyly	quickly
happily	wearily
tiredly	courageously
slowly	distinctly
sadly	cheerfully
clearly	miserably

2
a I sighed **unhappily**.

b The children spoke **quietly**.

c I put my clothes **untidily** on the chair.

d I did all my sums **correctly**.

e The nurse treated me **roughly**.

f The river flowed **slowly**.

g The boy spoke **rudely**.

h I did my writing **carefully**.

Unit 5: Revising syllables (page 39)

1
a poem   b lazy   c student
d label   e robot   f paper
g tidy   h stupid   i evil
j recent

2

First syllable ends with a long:				
a	e	i	o	u
lazy	evil	tidy	poem	student
label	recent		robot	stupid
paper				

3
a pu + pil   b si + lent
c a + corn   d o + pen
e di + et   f gra + vy
g la + ter   h po + ny
i du + ty   j ti + ger

Unit 6: Nouns – diminutives (page 40)

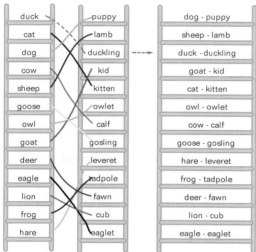

Unit 7: Confusing words (page 41)

1
a It will take me **two** seconds.
b It is **too** hard for me to do.
c I would like an ice cream **too**.
d I have written **two** letters.
e May I come **too**?
f The tree was **too** high to climb.
g It is **too** late to go out.
h You wear **two** socks.
i I have **two** pets.
j I feel **too** hot in the sun.

2
a I want **to** play the piano.
b I want to learn to play it **too**.
c Is it **too** difficult?
d You must go **to** a piano teacher **to** learn.

3 The **two** men tried **to** climb the mountain but it was **too** high.

Unit 8: Similes (page 42)

1
a sly   b slow   c slippery
d playful   e heavy   f strong
g busy   h hairy

2
a sweet   b smooth   c sharp
d flat   e cool   f red
g graceful   h dry

Unit 9: Prefixes – *in*, *im*, *il* and *ir* (page 43)

1
a incapable   b irresponsible
c immature   d illegible
e illegal   f irregular
g imperfect   h impatient
i inadequate   j inconsiderate

2
a illegal   b illegible
c irregular   d irresponsible
e incapable   f inadequate
g inconsiderate h immature
i impatient   j imperfect

3
a illogical   b inappropriate
c impractical   d irresistible
e incompetent   f inaccurate
g impertinent   h illiterate
i irrational   j incurable
k invisible   l improper

Unit 10: Writing sensible sentences (page 44)

1
a were   b were   c was   d were
e was   f were   g was   h were

2
a The apples that we ate were sweet.
b The children were very naughty.
c "I haven't done anything wrong!" the thief protested.
d The child did not take any notice of her teacher.
e Pass me those books, please.
f The instructor taught the woman how to drive.
g The girl threw her rubbish in the bin.
h I did 20 sums this morning.

Unit 11: Tricky spellings (page 45)

1
a guy   b rogue   c vague
d guitar   e guess   f guide

g guilty　　h plague　　i league
j catalogue

2

| begin with **gu** | guy | guitar | guess | guide | guilty |
| end with **gue** | rogue | vague | plague | league | catalogue |

3　a vague　　b guilty　　c guitar
　　d guy　　　e plague　　f guide
　　g guess　　h rogue　　i catalogue
　　j league

4　a dialogue　b disguise　c fatigue
　　d guarantee　e guard　　f guest
　　g intrigue　　h tongue

Unit 12: Revising pronouns (page 46)

1　a S　b S　c P　d P　e S
　　f S　g P　h S

2

a	b	c	d	m e	f	g
h	i	j	k	l	s h e
m	n	p	v	i t	w	x
t h e	y	z	x	c	v
c	d	e	h i m	f	h
i	j	o u r	m	n	b
q	w	t h e m	x	r
b	v	c	h e r	x	z

_me_ (singular)
she (singular)/_he_ (singular)
_it_ (singular)
they (plural)
him (singular)
our (plural)
them (plural)
her (singular)

Unit 13: Revising speech marks (page 47)

Teacher:　What's the matter, Tom?
Tom:　　 I am having trouble with my picture.
Teacher:　How can I help you?
Tom:　　 I can't seem to find the right green for this tree.
Teacher:　Have you tried mixing up some paints?
Tom:　　 Which colours do I mix to make green?
Teacher:　Try using some blue and yellow paint.
Tom:　　 Look! That's much better!
Teacher:　Well done!

Unit 14: Common word endings – *ar* (page 48)

1

beggar	someone who breaks into houses to steal
grammar	a sour liquid
cellar	someone who begs
burglar	someone who is in charge of a church
sugar	the rules of our language
vinegar	someone who studies at school
collar	a room underneath a house
vicar	a substance put in foods or drinks to sweeten them
scholar	a post that helps to hold up a building
pillar	the part of a shirt that goes round the neck

2

q	w	r e g u l a r	t	y	u		regular
z	x	c	v	f a m i l i a r		familiar
l	p a r t i c u l a r	m		particular
b	v	c	p o p u l a r	j	h		popular
d	r	m u s c u l a r	f	g		muscular
a	s	d	f	g	s i m i l a r		similar
c i r c u l a r	w	r	t	f		circular

Unit 15: Revising prepositions (page 49)

1　a th under　b s up ply　c sn at ch
　　d c off ee　e h over　　f on ly
　　g past ry　h w in dow

2　a in　b at　c under　d off　e past
　　f up　g on　h over

Unit 16: Letter patterns and sounds (page 50)

1　b**ough** t**ough** c**ough** r**ough**
　　thr**ough** tr**ough** th**ough** en**ough**
　　n**ough**t f**ough**t b**ough**t br**ough**t

2

		Rhymes with:			
port	stuff	zoo	toe	how	scoff
nought	tough	through	though	bough	cough
fought	rough				trough
bought	enough				
brought					

Unit 17: Joining sentences (page 51)

a　The hungry boy asked for a sandwich.
b　The kind man helped the old woman.
c　The brave woman rescued the drowning child.
d　The busy builder was laying some bricks.
e　The old car should not be on the road.
f　The young woman is wearing a lovely dress.

g The dirty windows need cleaning.
h The light case was easy to pick up.
i The tired boy could not run any further.
j The old castle stood on top of the hill.

Unit 18: Suffixes – *ness, hood, ship* (page 52)

① a ill**ness**　　　b child**hood**
　c dark**ness**　　　d friend**ship**
　e boy**hood**　　　f parent**hood**
　g bright**ness**　　h leader**ship**
　i sick**ness**　　　j sad**ness**
　k neighbour**hood**　l scholar**ship**
　m blind**ness**　　　n girl**hood**
　o hard**ness**/hard**ship**
　p quiet**ness**　　　q man**hood**
　r fellow**ship**　　s adult**hood**
　t good**ness**

②

-ness words	-hood words	-ship words
illness	childhood	friendship
darkness	boyhood	leadership
brightness	parenthood	scholarship
sickness	neighbourhood	hardship
sadness	girlhood	fellowship
blindness	manhood	
hardness	adulthood	
quietness		
goodness		

Unit 19: Apostrophes (page 53)

① a can't　　b didn't　　c I'm
　d you'll　　e they're　　f that's
　g don't　　h couldn't　i hadn't
　j he's

② a The letter **has not** come yet.
　b I **will not** do it again.
　c You **should not** run across a busy road.
　d **That is** my coat on the hook.
　e **There is** no-one at home.
　f **How is** your bad leg?
　g **We are** going out soon.
　h **You have** got a lovely smile.

Unit 20: Using a dictionary (page 54)

a cloud　　　　b steady
c scratch　　　d gardener
e interesting　f aeroplane
g swimming　　h writing
i joined　　　j noisy
k frightened　l awkward
m cupboard　　n square
o before　　　p treasure
q careful　　　r always
s should　　　t lorries

Test 1 (pages 55 and 56)

① a steal　　　　　b currant
② a will ride　　　b will go
③ a bri**dge**　　　b sle**dge**
④ a slowly　　　　b untidily
⑤ a ro + bot　　　b ti + ger
⑥ a gosling　　　　b duckling
⑦ a It is **too** far to walk.
　b I am going **to** the library.
⑧ a as <u>slow</u> as a snail
　b as <u>fast</u> as a cheetah
⑨ a **im**possible　　b **ir**regular
⑩ a We **were** late home.
　b I **was** reading a book.

Test 2 (pages 57 and 58)

① a guide　　　　　b tong**ue**
② a P　　　　　　　b S
③ Anna: Why are you unhappy?
　Dragon: My fire has gone out!
④ a vineg**ar**　　　b sug**ar**
⑤ a <u>D</u>over　　　b <u>S</u>underland
⑥ a c**ough**　　　b pl**ough**
⑦ a The tired woman went to bed.
　b The broken toy was on the floor.
⑧ a friend**ship**　b bright**ness**
⑨ a they're　　　b don't
⑩ a suddenly　　b scared or scarred